If Dragon Flies Made Honey

Poems collected by
DAVID KHERDIAN

Illustrated by
JOSE ARUEGO & ARIANE DEWEY

GREENWILLOW BOOKS
A Division of William Morrow & Company, Inc., New York

Library of Congress Cataloging in Publication Data
Main entry under title: If dragon flies made honey.
Summary: Includes twenty-five selections by contemporary poets.   1. Children's poetry.   [1. American poetry—Collections]   I. Kherdian, David.   II. Aruego, Jose.   III. Dewey, Ariane.
PN6110.C4I34   811'.5'408   77-3730   ISBN 0-688-80101-3   ISBN 0-688-84101-5 lib. bdg.

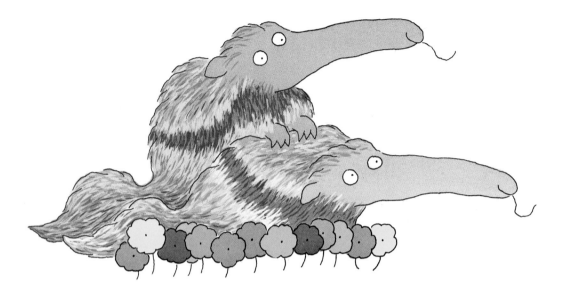

Grateful acknowledgment is made to the following for permission to include copyrighted poems:

Black Sparrow Press for Kenneth Gangemi's "Classroom," from his book *Lydia*, Copyright © 1970 by Kenneth Gangemi / Alvaro Cardona-Hine for "Garden Poem II," from his book *Words on Paper*, published by Red Hill Press, Copyright © 1974 by Alvaro Cardona-Hine / City Lights Books for the haiku from "Some Western Haikus" by Jack Kerouac, from his book *Scattered Poems*, Copyright © 1971 by the Estate of Jack Kerouac / Siv Cedering Fox for "In the Morning," Copyright © 1977 by Siv Cedering Fox / The Giligia Press for Ray Drew's poem from his *Goat Songs*, Copyright © 1970 by Ray Drew / Alfred Starr Hamilton for "Zounds" and "Town," from *The Poems of Alfred Starr Hamilton*, published by The Jargon Society, Copyright © 1970 by Alfred Starr Hamilton / Sam Hamod for "The Jealousy," from his book *The Holding Action*, published by The Seamark Press, Copyright © 1969 by H. Sam Hamod / The Jargon Society for "March" by Lorine Niedecker, from her *T & G (Collected Poems 1936-66)*, Copyright © 1969 by Lorine Niedecker / David Kherdian for "Outside the Supermarket" and "North Chatham Mud Pond Poem," Copyright © 1977 by David Kherdian / Ruth Krauss for "Weather," from her book *This Breast Gothic*, published by The Bookstore Press, Lenox, Mass., Copyright © 1973 by Ruth Krauss / Tom McKeown for "Orange," from his book *The Luminous Revolver*, published by The Sumac Press, Copyright © 1973 by Tom McKeown / Douglas J. McReynolds for "Waiting at the St. Louis Zoo," Copyright © 1977 by Douglas J. McReynolds / James Minor for "Giddy Up," and "Pine at Night Cry of the Owls," Copyright © 1975 by James Minor, published in *Stoney Lonesome #5*; and "Poplar," Copyright © 1973 by James Minor, published in *Gallery Series/Poets* by Harper Square Press / New Directions Publishing Corporation for Hayden Carruth's verse from his poem "North Winter" (#42), from his book *For You*, Copyright © 1964, 1970 by Hayden Carruth; for Charles Reznikoff's verse iii from "Autobiography: Hollywood," from his book *By the Waters of Manhattan*, Copyright 1941 by Charles Reznikoff; and for William Carlos Williams' "The Intelligent Sheepman and the New Cars," from his *Pictures from Brueghel*, Copyright © 1962 by William Carlos Williams / W. W. Norton & Company, Inc. for A. R. Ammons' "Poem" from his *Diversifications, Poems*, Copyright © 1975 by A. R. Ammons; and for his "Chasm," "Small Song," and "Mirrorment," from his *Collected Poems, 1951-1971*, Copyright © 1972 by A. R. Ammons / Rutgers University Press for John Stone's "Tree," from his book *The Smell of Matches*, Copyright © 1972 by Rutgers University, the State University of New Jersey.

Contents

GARDEN POEM II

if
dragon
flies
made
honey
their
honey
would
be
blue
and
you
would
have
two
whole
jars
of
it

ALVARO CARDONA-HINE

Boredom

I stare at
The number 2

I stare at
The number 2

I stare at
The number 2

It looks
Like a swan!

KENNETH GANGEMI

7   WEATHER

Whoops in the goobies and poosha tonight.
Sunday no poosha.

RUTH KRAUSS

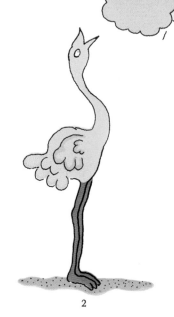

1

3

4

5

<pre>
8   gid   dy
     up   gid
     dy   up
     gid   dy   up
     gid   dy   up
     gid dy   up
     giddy   up
     giddy up   giddy up
     giddyup   giddyup
     giddyupgiddyupgiddyup
     giddyupgiddyupgiddyup
</pre>

JAMES MINOR

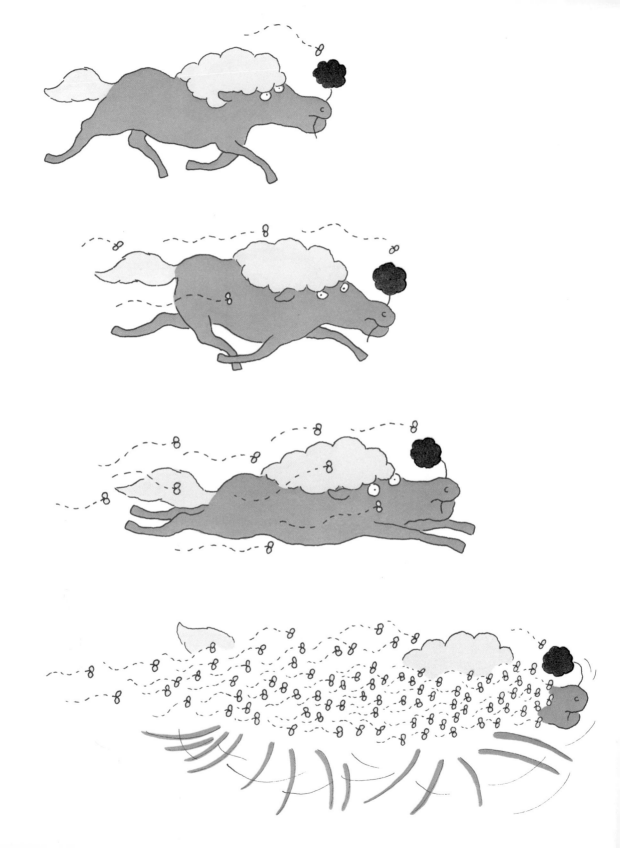

10 SMALL SONG

The reeds give
way to the

wind and give
the wind away

A. R. AMMONS

11　PINE AT NIGHT
CRY OF THE OWLS

O_VO

o_vo

JAMES MINOR

The
poplar
in
early
spring
looks
like
a
fish
skeleton
in
water

water
in
skeleton
fish
a
like
looks
spring
early
in
poplar
The

JAMES MINOR

In my medicine cabinet,
    the winter fly
has died of old age.

JACK KEROUAC

14   TREE

I was used to you
and your countable
branches.

What is this sudden
bursting into leaves?

JOHN STONE

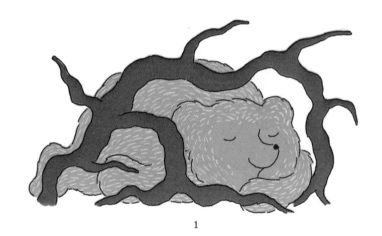

1

2

3

4

5

the man
carrying two
round
shopping bags
makes
(by his size)
a
third

DAVID KHERDIAN

17 THE JEALOUSY

The smell of this afternoon's rain
is driving the flowers crazy—

they're screaming for me to kiss them!

SAM HAMOD

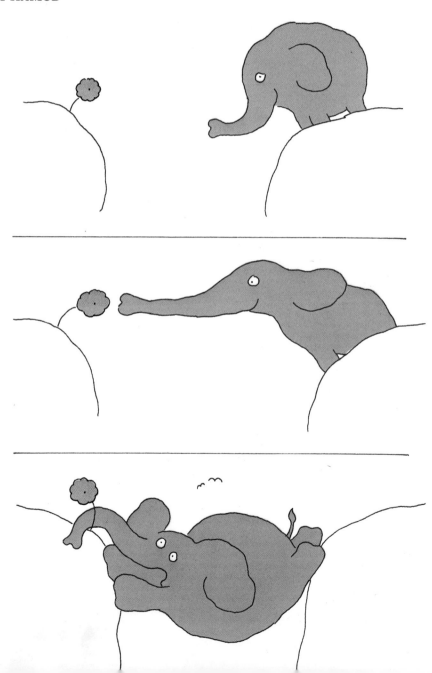

In a high wind the
leaves don't
fall but fly
straight out of the
tree like birds

A. R. AMMONS

19 ORANGE

more than a fruit
a word
a round word

the mouth makes
the orange sound

the color comes
after the sound

soars smoothly
across the room

TOM MC KEOWN

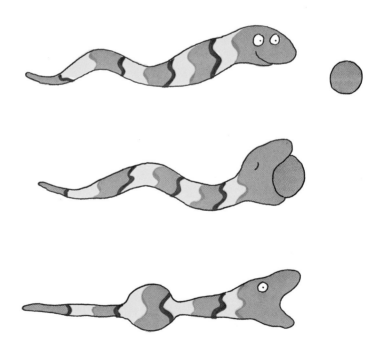

8 Turtles
on a log, glistening
    in the sun
—all in a row—

Number 4 turtle
slowly turns in a circle
stops, changes his mind,
and plops into the pond.

DAVID KHERDIAN

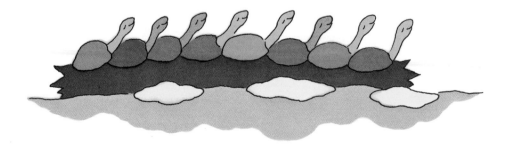

After I'd bought balloons and
made monkey faces from picnic chairs;
after I'd scratched the walrus chin
and climbed the stairs
into the snake house and trembled past
the lions' lairs,
I always came back to the bears.

DOUG MCREYNOLDS

23   from GOAT SONGS

Traveller approaching.
No. Moonlight on sunflower leaves.
Welcome him.

RAY DREW

But an old stone
That gathers moss
    Moans in the woodlands

ALFRED STARR HAMILTON

Snow's downstrokes climb softly up the c
                        i
                        n f
                        o e
                          r.

HAYDEN CARRUTH

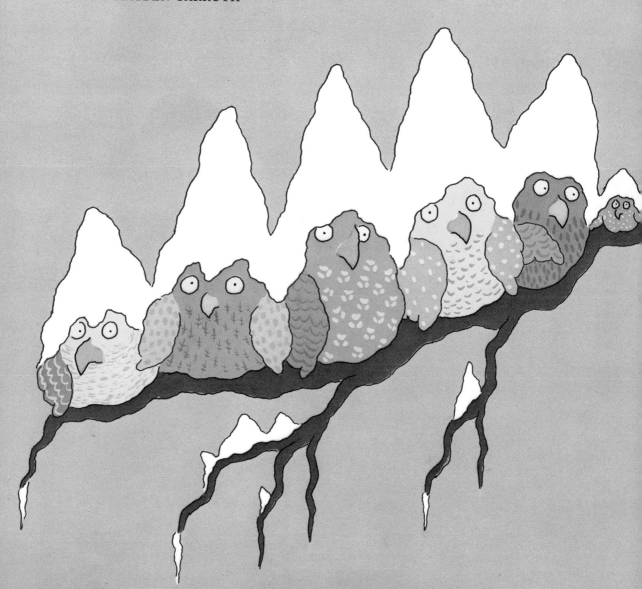

26 CHASM

Put your
self out
and you're
not quite
up to
it or
all in

A. R. AMMONS

a little bird
that has no name
flies
westward
pulling away
the dark blanket
of
the night

SIV CEDERING FOX

Give us time
Give us crickets
Give us a clock
could you build this wonderful town house in the grass
and put a cricket in it by this evening?

ALFRED STARR HAMILTON

I'd like to
pull
the back out

and use
one of them
to take

my "girls"
to
the fairs in

WILLIAM CARLOS WILLIAMS

30 MARCH

Bird feeder's
   snow-cap
      sliding
         off

LORINE NIEDECKER

I like this walk in the morning
among flowers and trees.
Only the birds are noisy.
But if they talk to me,
no matter how witty or wrong,
I do not have to answer;
and if they order me about,
I do not have to obey.

CHARLES REZNIKOFF

Birds are flowers flying
and flowers perched birds.

A. R. AMMONS